MMA

MMA

ODYSSEYS

JIM WHITING

CREATIVE EDUCATION · CREATIVE PAPERBACKS

Published by Creative Education and Creative Paperbacks
P.O. Box 227, Mankato, Minnesota 56002
Creative Education and Creative Paperbacks
are imprints of The Creative Company
www.thecreativecompany.us

Design by Blue Design (www.bluedes.com)
Production by Joe Kahnke
Printed in China

Photographs by Alamy (Dan Cooke, EDB Image Archive,
Entertainment Pictures, Francis Specker, United Archives
GmbH), Creative Commons Wikimedia (Sailko), Getty Images
(Allsport Hulton Archive/Stringer/Getty Images Sport Classic,
Markus Boesch/Getty Images Sport, David Dermer/Diamond
Images, Jeff Gross/Getty Images Sport, Jon P. Kopaloff/
Getty Images Sport, Steve Marcus/Stringer/Getty Images
Sport, Jared Wickerham/Getty Images Sport), iStockphoto
(miljko, Sergey_Peterman, vuk8691), Shutterstock (agusyonok,
antoniodiaz, Stefan Holm, Leeloona, LightField Studios)

Library of Congress Cataloging-in-Publication Data
Names: Whiting, Jim, author.
Title: MMA (Mixed martial arts) / Jim Whiting.
Series: Odysseys in extreme sports.
Includes bibliographical references and index.
Summary: An in-depth survey of the popular extreme sport
of mixed martial arts, from its roots in ancient Greece to its
televised matches, as well as its rules, methods, and famous
fighters.
Identifiers: LCCN 2017028047 / ISBN 978-1-60818-692-1
(hardcover) / ISBN 978-1-62832-288-0 (pbk) / ISBN 978-1-
56660-728-5 (eBook)

Subjects: LCSH: Mixed martial arts—Juvenile literature.
Classification: LCC GV1102.7.M59 W544 2018 / DDC 796.815—
dc23

CCSS: RI 8.1, 2, 3, 4, 5, 8, 10; RI 9-10.1, 2, 3, 4, 5, 8, 10; RI 11-12.1,
2, 3, 4, 5, 10; RST 6-8.1, 2, 5, 6, 10; RST 9-10.1, 2, 5, 6, 10; RST
11-12.1, 2, 5, 6, 10

First Edition HC 9 8 7 6 5 4 3 2 1
First Edition PBK 9 8 7 6 5 4 3 2 1

CONTENTS

Introduction

Soured on soccer? Fed up with football? Bored by baseball? Turned off by team sports? If so, extreme sports might be more to your liking. While there's not an exact definition of what makes a sport "extreme," the following characteristics (or at least most of them) seem to be common: a higher degree of risk despite use of protective gear, emphasis on achieving high speeds and/or

OPPOSITE: A sport that is growing in popularity, mixed martial arts allows participants to use a variety of moves, including submission holds, punching, and kicking.

heights, more likely to be performed alone or with a handful of friends, no issues with playing time as in team sports, stunts requiring substantial amounts of skill and practice, less emphasis on formal rules, and an **adrenaline** rush from physical exertion.

One of the United States' fastest-growing sports is Mixed **Martial Arts** (MMA). Some of its characteristics differ from other extreme sports. For example, MMA participants must follow strict rules and have formal coaching. Otherwise, they could be seriously injured. Part of what makes MMA extreme is how far the participants are pushed physically. Also, during its early years, many people regarded it as a violent and brutal activity outside the bounds of traditional sports. Some of this negative image still remains, adding to its extreme reputation.

A Martial Arena

MMA could be thought of as one of the world's oldest—and yet newest—sports. The "oldest" part dates back to the ancient Greek Olympics. In 648 B.C., a sport called pankration was introduced to the Games. Pankration combined elements of boxing and wrestling— both of which were already Olympic sports—and added kicking and just about anything else to disable an opponent. Two things

Winner: The Dead Guy

At the Olympics in 564 B.C., Arrichion of the ancient Greek city
of Phigalia was favored to win the pankration event. He'd easily
taken the title during the two previous Games. During the final
match, Arrichion's opponent—who was never identified by
name—leaped on his back, wrapped his legs around Arrichion's
legs, and began choking him. With his last reserves of strength,
Arrichion kicked out and toppled over in such a way that the
opponent dislocated his ankle. The man screamed in pain
and immediately raised his hand to signal his surrender. But
Arrichion was dead—of suffocation, a broken neck brought
about by the fall, or perhaps even a **congenital** heart condition.
The judges conferred briefly and declared Arrichion the victor.

were off-limits: biting and eye-gouging. It was an especially brutal sport. Serious injuries (and the occasional death) were regarded as "part of the game." Despite this reputation—or perhaps because of it—pankration became the most popular event of the Games, with a boys division added in 200 B.C.

Greek foot soldiers were familiar with pankration. Some historians believe that the Greek conqueror Alexander the Great introduced the sport to India in the 320s B.C. From there, they say, it spread into other parts of Asia. What is certain is that a number of martial arts can trace their origins to Asian countries.

Karate developed on the island of Okinawa in response to the Japanese takeover of the island in the late 19th century. Meaning "empty hands" in Japanese, karate uses the hands and feet to deliver blows and block attacks.

The roots of jujitsu are found in 15th-century Japan. This form of unarmed combat originated in situations where conventional weapons were ineffective. Translated as "the art of gentleness," it differs from other martial arts in its use of an opponent's own weight to hurl him to the ground and immobilize him.

Muay Thai, which originated in Thailand, is known as "the art of eight limbs." Practitioners are trained to use their fists, elbows, shins, and knees.

From Korea came tae kwon do ("art of hand and foot fighting"). It is especially noted for its aggressive use of kicking.

An **offshoot** of jujitsu, judo was founded in Japan in the late 1800s by Jigoro Kano. Judo became a way of life in addition to its value as a martial art. To promote his new sport, Kano sent its leading practitioner, Mitsuyo

Maeda, on a world tour in 1904. At only 5-foot-5 and 155 pounds, Maeda created a sensation by consistently defeating much larger men. In more than 2,000 fights, he lost just twice.

Maeda eventually settled in Brazil, where he befriended the Gracie family and passed along his techniques. The Gracies, in turn, originated a fighting style known as Brazilian jujitsu. It focuses on ground fighting and grappling holds.

In 1978, Rorion Gracie moved to the U.S. and began teaching Brazilian jujitsu. A decade later, a magazine article termed him "the toughest man in America." Advertising executive Art Davie saw the article, and he partnered with Gracie to publicize the sport. On November 12, 1993, they staged "the Ultimate Fighting Championship" (UFC), matching eight prominent

A grappling-based martial art, Brazilian jujitsu is known for its ground-fighting elements and focuses on using holds to gain leverage on opponents.

fighters from a variety of disciplines. Televised only on **pay-per-view**, it drew more than 86,000 viewers.

The co-promoters knew that television was important and that they needed to create a new image for the sport. "From the moment it appeared on television, it couldn't look like what we were preconditioned to assume was just another fight," said Michael Pillot, one of the men who helped plan the competition. "We needed the viewer to look at this in a completely different way."

That meant staging a "completely different" arena.

"From the moment it appeared on television, it couldn't look like what we were preconditioned to assume was just another fight."

Early ideas on how to do this were extreme. "We thought of a moat with alligators," Rorion Gracie recalled. "We thought of an arena with sharks around. We seriously thought about an electric fence. But we couldn't in case one guy pushed the other into the moat and he'd get chewed up."

On a more realistic level, the organizers needed a structure that wouldn't give anyone an advantage because of familiarity. Boxers, for example, were accustomed to fighting in a square ring, while serious wrestlers competed inside a circle.

Eventually they came up with the now-legendary eight-sided arena known as the Octagon. It's a raised

On the check:

W.O.W. PROMOTIONS™

5045

12 NOV 19 93

$50,000

The Ultimate Fighter!

Fifty Thousand ——————— DOLLARS

00
XX

UFC 1

UFC 1 was held at McNichols Sports Arena in Denver, Colorado. Eight men from a variety of martial arts took part in a tournament with three rounds. There were no weight classes or judges. The first round had four fights, with the winners meeting in the semifinals. Those two winners competed in the final, in which Royce Gracie (the tournament's smallest fighter and Rorion's brother) defeated Dutch karate specialist Gerard Gordeau. Gracie went on to win UFC 2 and UFC 4. The fact that UFC continued was a surprise to the organizers. As UFC president Dana White explained, the fight "was only supposed to be a **one-off**. Well, it did so well on pay-per-view they decided to do another, and another. Never in a million years did these guys think they were creating a sport."

platform measuring up to 30 feet (9.1 m) from side to side. The angles at each corner are wider than those of a square, preventing fighters from getting trapped. Six-foot-high (1.8 m) fencing up to a padded top keeps the fighters from being hurled out of the ring. The surface is canvas.

That fight—now known as UFC 1—was successful and spawned several televised sequels. But not everyone was excited about this extreme fighting format. Arizona senator John McCain was appalled at the violence. He called it "human cockfighting" and urged every state to ban it. Most did. In response, UFC began adding and changing its rules. Within a few years, most of the current standards were in place, and the sport resumed its upward climb. However, the years of struggle had been costly. The original promoters were nearly bankrupt. Two brothers, Lorenzo and Frank Fertitta, and their friend Dana White had become UFC fans. They formed Zuffa, LLC and bought UFC in 2001 for $2 million. White became the president.

n 2005, Zuffa persuaded Spike TV to air *The Ultimate Fighter*, a reality series in which established fighters train up-and-coming young talent. It soon became Spike's top-rated show and ran on that channel through 2011. It was then moved to the Fox Sports 1 network. Throughout the 2000s, more people began watching UFC bouts on television and in-person. Although other MMA organizations have arisen, UFC remains the most significant and its champions the most well-known. Many fighters from other MMA organizations have joined UFC, making it even stronger.

By 2016, UFC as a company was valued at more than $2 billion. Because of its success, many people regard MMA as an integral part of the contemporary sports scene, and even casual observers are familiar with its biggest names.

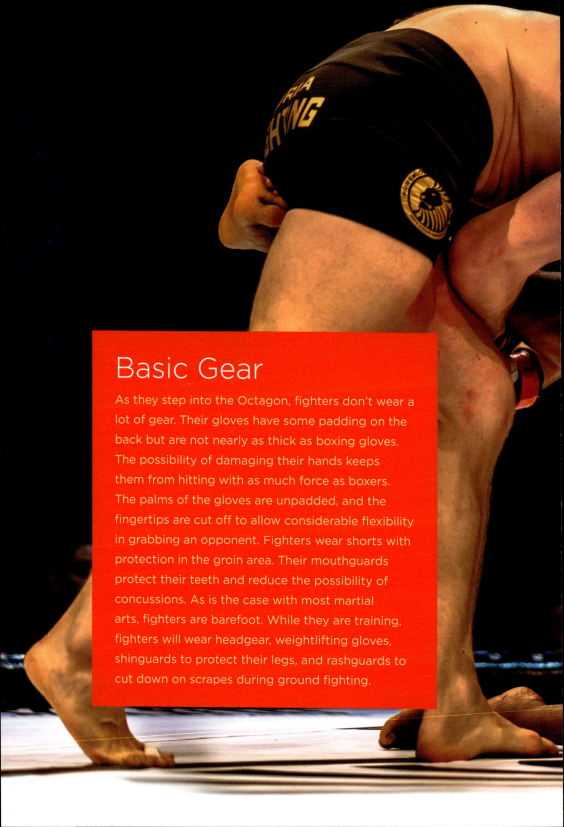

Basic Gear

As they step into the Octagon, fighters don't wear a lot of gear. Their gloves have some padding on the back but are not nearly as thick as boxing gloves. The possibility of damaging their hands keeps them from hitting with as much force as boxers. The palms of the gloves are unpadded, and the fingertips are cut off to allow considerable flexibility in grabbing an opponent. Fighters wear shorts with protection in the groin area. Their mouthguards protect their teeth and reduce the possibility of concussions. As is the case with most martial arts, fighters are barefoot. While they are training, fighters will wear headgear, weightlifting gloves, shinguards to protect their legs, and rashguards to cut down on scrapes during ground fighting.

A Real Knockout

MMA fighters master skills in five key
areas: striking, the clinch, takedowns,
ground fighting, and submission holds.
Striking closely resembles boxing,
and it's how most matches begin.
The fighters rush toward each other
and exchange blows. Sometimes a
match ends here, as one fighter lands
a punch that knocks out his opponent.
He may also do enough damage
with a series of blows to result in a
technical knockout (TKO).

OPPOSITE: People trained in the art of Muay Thai specialize in
using eight points of contact—their fists, elbows, shins, and knees—
on opponents. For this reason, Muay Thai is also called "the art of
eight limbs."

There are several different types of punches, including the following: A jab is a short, powerful blow in which the fighter snaps his lead hand (left for a right-handed fighter, right for a lefty) in a straight line toward his opponent. It's not usually a knockout punch, but it can set up more devastating blows. A cross is a punch in which the rear hand crosses in front of the fighter's face and connects with the opponent's jaw with the full force of the fighter's body weight behind it. To employ an uppercut, the fighter's fist begins at about waist level and targets the opponent's chin. A hook is a punch in which the lead hand travels in a circular motion rather than in a straight line, as is the case with a jab. An overhead is a rear-hand punch that arches above the fighter's head before making contact with the opponent. Different punches are often used in combination. For example, a series of quick jabs can distract an opponent, leaving him open to a devastating cross.

I n addition to using their hands, fighters draw from other martial arts and strike with their elbows, legs, feet, and knees. One of the sport's most spectacular moments comes when a fighter delivers a roundhouse kick that knocks the opponent to the mat.

In MMA, a clinch helps a fighter land hard strikes. This differs from boxing. In boxing, a clinch occurs when two fighters move in close and wrap their arms around each other. It provides a brief opportunity to

Fighters can win a UFC contest in one of three ways: knocking out an opponent, forcing the opponent to submit or "tap out," or tallying enough points to earn the victory.

rest rather than fight. Referees quickly break it up. One clinch technique in MMA is called "dirty boxing." The fighter grabs the back of his opponent's head and pulls it down with one hand while throwing short-range punches (usually hooks and uppercuts) with the other. Many knee and elbow strikes occur in clinches. Fighters also try to deliver short, sharp punches to their opponent's midsection. Clinches are often the prelude to a takedown.

n its simplest form, a takedown occurs when one fighter takes the opponent to the mat. There are many ways to do this. One of the most common is the single-leg takedown. The fighter grabs one of his opponent's legs with both hands and lifts it as high as he can. While the opponent struggles to balance on his remaining leg, the fighter drives him to the mat.

Another common method is the double-leg takedown. The fighter quickly drops down and takes a step between his opponent's legs, driving his shoulder into the opponent's midsection. This forces the other fighter's chest over the attacker. The attacker then grabs his opponent's legs and drives forward, toppling him onto the mat.

Perhaps the most spectacular takedown is the body slam. The fighter gains complete control of his opponent, lifts him into the air, and hurls him to the mat. The opponent is often stunned by the force of the fall, and savvy fighters take quick advantage of the situation.

A takedown marks the start of ground fighting, the

next phase of an MMA match. Ground fighting refers to what happens when one or both fighters are on the mat. MMA fighters need to learn many ways of gaining control over their opponents during this phase. They also need effective means of defense.

One common technique in ground fighting is the "ground and pound," often used by fighters with strong wrestling backgrounds. It refers to forcing an opponent to the mat, straddling his chest, and then pummeling him with a series of hard punches.

These punches may end the fight or at least weaken the opponent and set him up for defeat by some other method.

Wrestlers tend to avoid being flipped onto their backs, as this is how they can be pinned and thereby lose the match. However, it can be an advantageous position in MMA, if the fighter can wrap his legs around his opponent. Many MMA fights end with the winner on his back.

The primary intention in ground fighting is to secure a submission hold. This brings the fight to a close. There are three general types of submission holds (with many variations of each type). One is choking an opponent to the point where breathing becomes difficult. Another is a joint lock. This involves putting intense pressure on an opponent's joint. In an armbar joint lock, for example, a fighter locks the opponent's arm between his legs and twists to put painful pressure on the elbow. The third

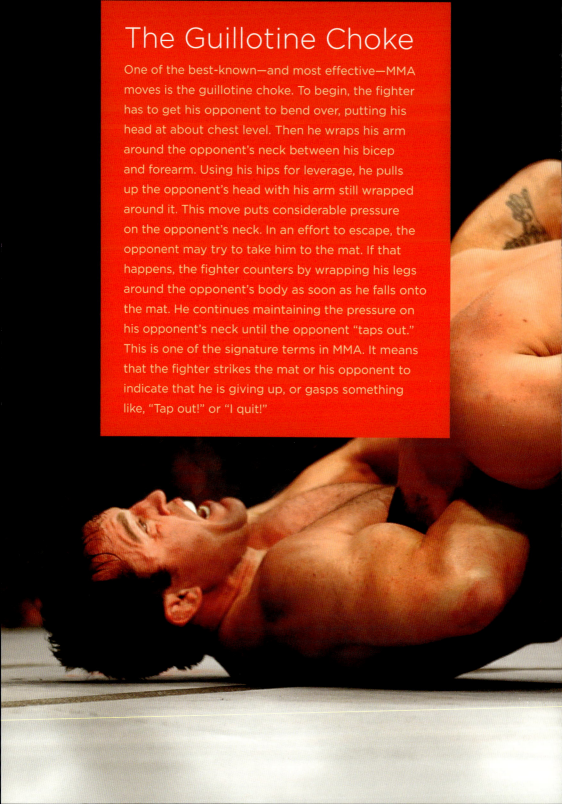

The Guillotine Choke

One of the best-known—and most effective—MMA moves is the guillotine choke. To begin, the fighter has to get his opponent to bend over, putting his head at about chest level. Then he wraps his arm around the opponent's neck between his bicep and forearm. Using his hips for leverage, he pulls up the opponent's head with his arm still wrapped around it. This move puts considerable pressure on the opponent's neck. In an effort to escape, the opponent may try to take him to the mat. If that happens, the fighter counters by wrapping his legs around the opponent's body as soon as he falls onto the mat. He continues maintaining the pressure on his opponent's neck until the opponent "taps out." This is one of the signature terms in MMA. It means that the fighter strikes the mat or his opponent to indicate that he is giving up, or gasps something like, "Tap out!" or "I quit!"

submission hold is the compression lock, in which a fighter presses a muscle tightly against the bone. Two common compression locks are the bicep slicer and the leg slicer. When an opponent can no longer deal with the pain and discomfort of a submission hold, he taps out.

Many fighters have a particular specialty. They come to MMA after establishing themselves in a martial art. They then need to learn at least the basics of other martial arts to level the playing field. With so many disciplines to master, it's not surprising that fighters spend long hours in training. In addition to working on hundreds of individual techniques, they also must build strength and stamina. It's not uncommon for them to work out twice daily for two to three hours each time.

Fighting for a Place

Hélio Gracie was so scrawny that he had to drop out of school in his native Brazil in the second grade. He learned jujitsu by observing classes taught by his older brother Carlos. One day, Carlos didn't show up for a private lesson. Hélio, then 16, offered to step in. The student liked Hélio so much that he asked him to continue as his teacher.

Aided by a diet that Carlos

developed for him, Hélio used his teaching experiences to become stronger. But he still lacked the upper-body strength to be successful in jujitsu. So he focused on ground fighting, using his legs to control his opponents, even though many of them significantly outweighed him.

Hélio's new system became known as *vale tudo*, which is loosely translated as "no holds barred." He took on challengers in matches so popular they had to be staged in soccer stadiums. In Brazil, vale tudo became second only to soccer in spectator interest.

Hélio fought for more than 25 years. One of his most memorable bouts came when he was 42. He took on a former student, Waldemar Santana, in a fight that lasted nearly four hours without a break. It ended when Santana kicked Hélio in the head. Hélio's final fight came 13 years later, in 1967, when he forced his opponent to submit.

nother key figure in the development of MMA was actor and martial artist Bruce Lee. UFC president Dana White called Lee the "father of mixed martial arts" because he was among the first to combine several types of fighting. Lee was born in San Francisco in 1940 and raised in Hong Kong, China, where he appeared in nearly 20 films. As a teenager, he began studying Asian martial arts. He also became a good boxer and even learned to **fence**.

When Lee was 18, he returned to the U.S. He wanted to become one of the world's best fighters, so he added even more skills. He also emphasized nutrition and the spiritual side of life.

He revived his acting career and moved back to Hong Kong, which had a thriving martial arts film industry.

Lee quickly became its biggest star. His most famous film was *Enter the Dragon*. Tragically, he died suddenly only weeks before its release in 1973. In recognition of his accomplishments, in 1999 *Time* magazine named Bruce Lee among the 100 most important people of the 20th century.

R andy Couture was one of the first big names in MMA as it moved from a fringe sport into the mainstream. A wrestler in high school and college as well as a member of the elite 101st Airborne Division, Couture was an

alternate on the U.S. Olympic wrestling team in 1988, 1992, and 1996.

Couture's first UFC fight was in May 1997. By year's end he was heavyweight champion and nicknamed "The Natural." He left UFC soon afterward in a contract dispute and was stripped of his title. He returned late in 2000 and regained that title. After successive losses to much heavier opponents, he dropped down to the light heavyweight division in 2003. He won that championship as well, becoming the first fighter to win titles in two divisions. Couture retired in 2006 but made a comeback the following year when he was 43. Though he was competing against much younger fighters, he won the heavyweight championship again. He retired for good in 2011.

As Couture was leaving UFC, Anderson Silva was

reaching the peak of his own career. Silva grew up in poverty in Brazil, spending much of his early life with his aunt and uncle. He became interested in Brazilian jujitsu at a young age, though he couldn't afford lessons for several years. He made quick progress when his family's finances improved and he could receive formal training.

Silva turned pro in 1997 at the age of 22 and spent nearly a decade fighting in several MMA organizations, racking up a 9-match winning streak between 2000 and 2003. That set the stage for his joining UFC in 2006. He quickly launched a 16-bout winning streak, the longest in MMA history. It ended in 2013.

Many people think Silva is the greatest MMA fighter of all time. UFC broadcast analyst Joe Rogan says, "Anderson Silva is the best fighter on the planet and has been for a very long time. He is a bad, bad dude. The guys on his record—Rich Franklin, Dan Henderson, Forrest Griffin, Vitor Belfort—are a murderers' row of the best fighters in the world, and not one of them even got out of the second round with this guy."

hile MMA is still primarily a male sport, an increasing number of women are now being featured in bouts. As one of the first women to gain recognition in MMA, Gina Carano was called the "face of women's MMA." Before a 2008 fight, Carano said, "It's been unbelievable to be at

Former UFC middleweight champion Anderson Silva (left) boasts the longest title streak in UFC history, winning 16 consecutive fights from 2006 to 2012.

the forefront of women's MMA. Raising the recognition of the sport has been a blessing. The fan support has been amazing. I'm standing up here because of the fans."

Carano began her martial arts career in Muay Thai. Her then boyfriend Kevin Ross was a rising star in the sport, and Carano watched his training sessions. Ross's trainer said, "Hey, baby, you need to train; you're too fat; you need to train." Carano began training and eventually compiled a record of 12-1-1. In 2006, she was invited to participate in Nevada's first sanctioned women's MMA bout, winning by a knockout. Three years later, she was on the first **fight card** in which women were the featured bout, though she lost by a TKO.

By then her film career was underway and she had appeared in numerous roles. Fans hoped she would nevertheless return to the Octagon someday.

After a mostly successful string of MMA fights in the 2000s, Gina Carano (right) moved to the big screen, where she has appeared in several movies.

Mainstream MMA

As MMA moves farther into the mainstream of American sports, it has taken a stronger hold on pop culture. There is certainly no shortage of MMA books. Many deal with techniques, biographies of noted fighters, and other aspects of the sport. For example, *MMA Greats* (2012) by Lori Polydoros profiles several of the biggest names in the sport. Patrick Jones's *Ultimate Fighting: The Brains and*

Brawn of Mixed Martial Arts (2014) recounts the history of the sport and suggests some of the directions it may take in the future. Other educational books for young readers provide similar information.

Some works of fiction draw on MMA-related themes. In James McCann's *Flying Feet* (2010), for example, the main character Jinho is expelled from his tae kwon do training hall after breaking an opponent's fingers. An underground MMA club asks him to join, but Jinho finds that membership in the group is accompanied by its own set of issues.

Collaborating under the pen name of former wrestling promoter Jack Tunney, several authors have written the series Fight Card: MMA, though some of the content is more suitable for mature readers. *The Kalamazoo Kid* (2013) deals with former fighter Ray Kurt, who has become a trainer. He has high hopes for Tallis Dunbar, but his **protégé** runs afoul of the mob. In *Welcome to the Octagon* (2014), Mickey "The Rage" Rafferty needs to support his eight-year-old daughter. The best way he can make money is fighting in underground bouts. His trainer wants him to go legit, but that won't be easy. *Rosie the Ripper* (2014) takes a look into the world of female MMA fighters through the eyes of Rosie Bratton. Her life is seemingly on a downward spiral until a trainer named Felix—a former top-rated MMA fighter—believes that she can create a better life for herself by taking up the sport.

The Jake Maddox Sports Stories series includes books about various disciplines that compose MMA. In *Karate Countdown* (2009), a character named Kenny is angry all the time. His father signs him up for karate classes in an effort to focus his energies onto something positive. It's not an easy process, as Kenny soon learns. He might have to miss an important competition because the problem keeps flaring up. Anger issues also lie at the heart of *Takedown* (2009), in which the captain of the school's wrestling team invites Jeff to join the squad. Jeff needs to learn how to control his hot temper so he can succeed as a wrestler.

artial arts films have attracted moviegoers for several decades. While the late Bruce Lee is perhaps the most well-known figure in this **genre**, Chuck

Norris was also very popular. In somewhat of a coincidence, he starred in *The Octagon* in 1980. However, the film's title refers to a terrorist training camp rather than a UFC arena, and Norris plays a retired karate champion who takes down the terrorist group.

Like Lee, Norris was a genuine martial arts practitioner, rather than an actor who learned a few moves to make his movies seem credible. In 2014, he said, "Of course MMA wasn't in existence when Bruce [Lee] and I were training, and when I was fighting ... I have to say, being confident in myself, that I feel I would have done very well in the MMA arena, because of my judo training, I was a black belt in judo, plus I had multiple black belts in karate, tae kwon do, ... and so forth. Plus I studied jujitsu."

The increasing popularity of MMA has led to the

production of numerous MMA-specific movies in the past few years. Released in 2012, *Here Comes the Boom* takes a somewhat lighthearted approach to its subject. Scott Voss (played by Kevin James) is a former college wrestler who is now a bored high school teacher. The music program at his school is about to be cut for lack of funds, which would also result in his friend and colleague, Marty (Henry Winkler) losing his job. Voss learns that an upcoming MMA tournament will award enough money to the winner to cover the cost of maintaining the music program. The school nurse Bella (Salma Hayek) provides romantic interest and encourages Voss in his training and the big fight. *Here Comes the Boom* was named one of the 10 best family films by the 21st Annual Movieguide Awards, which described it as "a story of sacrifice and taking personal risk to help someone else."

At the other end of the **spectrum** is *Warrior* (2011).
Estranged brothers Tommy Conlon (Tom Hardy) and
Brendan Conlon (Joel Edgerton) enter an MMA tournament, in which they meet in the final match. Nick Nolte
plays the brothers' father and was nominated for Best
Supporting Actor Oscar. Though the film didn't do well
at the box office, most critics praised it. Many compared
it with *Rocky* (1976). Roger Ebert called it a "rich, seamy
drama of a troubled family.... This is a rare fight movie
in which we don't want to see either fighter lose. That
brings such complexity to the final showdown that hardly
anything could top it—but something does, and *Warrior*
earns it." Part of director Gavin O'Connor's emphasis in
making the film was to honor American servicepeople.
Tommy's character was an ex-Marine and many real-life
Marines served as extras during filming.

With its continuous action and variety of moves, MMA is an ideal subject for video games. In 2009, THQ, Inc. released *UFC Undisputed* for Xbox 360 and PlayStation 3. It was named the Best Individual Sports Game at the 2009 Spike Video Game Awards. Two sequels followed in quick succession. In 2014, *EA Sports UFC* made its debut. The game features nearly 100 active fighters as well as "bonus fighters" Royce Gracie and Bruce Lee. *EA Sports UFC* 2, released two years later, boasted improved graphics and an updated roster. Many fans were disappointed that the third installment of the game did not include Chuck Norris.

Healthy, Wealthy, and . . . Violent?

The experiences of UFC president Dana White can serve as a **microcosm** for the sport's development and likely future. In a 2010 article about UFC in *Esquire* magazine, journalist Mark Sager wrote, "Fifteen years ago, White was riding his bike through the slushy winter streets of Boston with eighty pounds of equipment in a hockey bag on his back, going from gym to gym to train his fitness clients.... [Today]

OPPOSITE: Under the leadership of president Dana White, both the UFC and MMA fighting have enjoyed an explosion in popularity and participation.

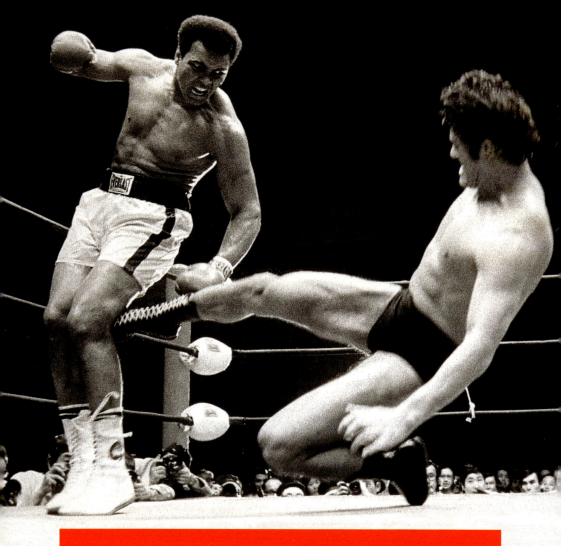

The Joke That Wasn't Funny

In 1975, world heavyweight champion boxer Muhammad Ali jokingly asked, "Isn't there any Oriental fighter to challenge me? I'll give him $1 million if he wins." Japanese wrestler Antonio Inoki took Ali up on his offer the following year in what is regarded as an early form of MMA. Limited by the special rules for the bout, Inoki spent most of the 15 rounds on his back, kicking out at Ali. Ali kept trying to dodge the kicks and landed only six punches in the entire fight. It was ruled a draw. Angry fans littered the ring with garbage. However, Inoki had landed enough kicks to open up several wounds on Ali's legs. They became infected and Ali nearly had to have one leg removed. He was never the same afterward.

White flies around in one of several company jets, stays in palatial suites at luxury hotels.... His thoughts on Twitter are followed by more than 800,000 people." He is a multimillionaire, as are his former Zuffa partners. (Zuffa sold UFC to WWE-IMG for nearly $4 billion in 2016.) That wealth extends to the UFC fighters. The top names often earn six figures for a fight. And it's likely that MMA will become even more popular and profitable in the future.

One ongoing question regards whether the sport will ever be accepted into the Olympics, often considered the pinnacle of sports. Resistance to its inclusion goes back more than a century. As the Baron Pierre de Coubertin and his fellow European nobles were making plans to revive the Olympics in 1896, an influential French priest named Pierre-Hector Coullié said, "We accept all [ancient events to be reinstated], except pankration."

This statement was misleading, however. Shooting, tennis, cycling, and even the marathon run weren't part of the original Olympics. And the modern Games don't include chariot racing. But Coullié's sentiment may still endure. As MMA blogger Josh Rosenblatt pointed out before the 2012 Summer Olympics in London, England, "fans of the Olympics can watch athletes competing in many of the disciplines that make up mixed martial arts—wrestling, boxing, judo, and tae kwon do—but not mixed martial arts itself. This is one of the great ironies of MMA: take the time and effort to master one fighting style and you're revered; take the time and effort to master all of them and you're an animal."

This situation may change at some point in the not-too-distant future. The growing international popularity of MMA—which translates into many more potential spectators—could become a factor. In 2014, Randy Couture, who remained active in the sport even after his retirement from fighting, commented that more than 30 countries have signed petitions urging its addition.

If MMA does become a part of the Olympics, it's likely that it would include both sexes. Wrestling for girls has become widespread at both the middle school and high school levels. Many U.S. states now have championship tournaments. In the same way, more women have been attracted to MMA, though they currently represent a small fraction of total viewership. However, an early pay-per-view bout between two women was so successful that servers became overloaded and the fight had to be streamed for free, with refunds issued. "With women, they come to fight," says Shannon Knapp, who promotes female fighters. "They'll fight just to show up. Even the way women get on social-media platforms to promote it, you can see how they'll push it more than the men will."

nother sign of the increasing participation of women and their appeal was UFC 184 in February 2015. The featured fight was the bantamweight title bout between Ronda Rousey and Cat Zingano. Both fighters were unbeaten going into the match. Rousey, a judo bronze medalist in the 2008 Olympics, was regarded

as the best female fighter on a pound-for-pound basis.

Rousey used an armbar to force Zingano to tap out in just 14 seconds, the fastest finish in UFC title bout history. "We were expecting that she might come out and do something flying at me right away," Rousey said. "That's not usually how you land an armbar at that angle, but it works. It was a lot like judo transitions, where you scramble the second you hit the ground. I made that up on the fly, to be honest."

Not everyone approves of this trend. Some male fighters claim that women are replacing them in what they regard as their "rightful place" on fight cards. There is also a lingering prejudice that it's "unladylike" to participate in such a brutal sport. And women have to put up with comments that no male fighters would ever encounter. As Zingano—who is also a mother—explains,

"People don't talk about [longtime UFC welterweight champion] Georges St. Pierre being hot.... They talk about how he's the baddest man alive."

Another issue regards the participation of young people. According to a market study in 2011, some 5 million teenagers and more than 3 million youngsters aged 13 and under participate in the sport. This represents a huge growth for an activity that barely registered in the national consciousness just two decades ago.

Not everyone is comfortable with this trend. Some people object to the culture of violence they believe MMA encourages. Others object to boys and girls fighting each other until the age of 12, when the sexes are separated. There is also the risk of concussions, especially since no one wears protective headgear.

Certain rules help safeguard young MMA fighters. Potentially dangerous takedowns are banned. So is hitting an opponent in the head. And advocates claim that no one has ever been seriously injured. They also point out that sports such as hockey and football, which include high-speed, bone-rattling collisions, don't seem to be subjected to the same kind of criticism. Equally important, kids are continually reminded that learning MMA isn't a license to bully. The exact opposite is true—it can be seen as a way of responding to bullies.

Another area of concern to some people is the possibility of boys fighting girls. But as one parent noted, "This sport boosts [my daughter's] self-confidence and self-esteem. When she fights boys and beats them, she can say to herself, 'I can do this.' She gets a huge sense of accomplishment with every win."

Many people also believe that MMA passes along valuable life lessons. The same parent continued, "MMA teaches her to work hard. She understands that being a winner takes dedication and focus. She realizes that to get such good results she has to put in the effort."

Many people, both inside the Octagon and out, have "put in the effort" to get MMA where it is today. It seems likely to surpass other combat sports such as boxing and wrestling in popularity and importance. And no one refers to it anymore as "human cockfighting."

Glossary

adrenaline   a substance produced by the body, often when physically or emotionally stressed, characterized by increased blood flow and heightened excitement

congenital   a trait, illness, or medical condition present from the time a person is born

estranged   no longer close to someone; often feeling bitter or angry toward that person

fence   to fight with swords as a sport with a strict set of rules

fight card   all the bouts that occur as part of the same event, most commonly during the course of a single evening

genre   a type of art such as movies or literature, with many similarities such as style or subject matter

martial arts   forms of combat or sports in which participants are unarmed and use their hands, feet, and other body parts to attack an opponent or defend themselves from that opponent

microcosm   something small regarded as having the same features or qualities as something else that is much larger

offshoot	something that originates from something else and develops in its own way
one-off	something happening once and not repeated
pay-per-view	cable television service in which subscribers pay to watch a particular event
protégé	a person who is guided and directed by someone older and more experienced
sequels	types of works that continue themes from an original version
spectrum	a scale of related items

Selected Bibliography

Couture, Randy. *The Best of Mixed Martial Arts: The Extreme Handbook on Techniques, Conditioning and the Smash-Mouth World of MMA*. Chicago: Triumph Books, 2008.

D'Souza, Brian J. *Pound for Pound: The Modern Gladiators of Mixed Martial Arts*. Toronto: Thracian, 2012.

Franklin, Rich, and Jon F. Merz. *The Complete Idiot's Guide to Ultimate Fighting*. Indianapolis, Ind.: Alpha Books, 2007.

Gentry, Clyde, III. *No Holds Barred: The Complete History of Mixed Martial Arts in America*. Chicago: Triumph Books, 2011.

Indio, Danny. *Mixed Martial Arts Fighting Techniques: Apply the Modern Training Methods Used by MMA Pros!* Rutland, Vt.: Tuttle, 2012.

Rooney, Martin. *Training for Warriors: The Ultimate Mixed Martial Arts Workout*. New York: HarperCollins, 2008.

Shamrock, Frank. *Mixed Martial Arts for Dummies.* With Mary Van Note. Hoboken, N.J.: Wiley, 2009.

Sobie, Brian, and Adam Elliott Segal. *MMA Now!: The Stars and Stories of Mixed Martial Arts*. Richmond Hill, Ont., Canada: Firefly Books, 2014.

Websites

How the Ultimate Fighting Championship Works
https://entertainment.howstuffworks.com/ufc1.htm

This overview of UFC includes basic information, fighting techniques, a brief history, a look at the future, and numerous links for additional information.

Ultimate Fighting Championship
http://www.ufc.com/

The official UFC website includes news, fighter biographies, previews of upcoming fights, results, photos and videos, merchandise, and more.

Note: Every effort has been made to ensure that any websites listed above were active at the time of publication. However, because of the nature of the Internet, it is impossible to guarantee that these sites will remain active indefinitely or that their contents will not be altered.

Index